Wildflower hotspots

T he Wildlife Trusts (WT) maintain more than 2250 nature reserves. These look after all the wildlife habitats found in the UK, from wildflower meadows and ancient woodlands to estuaries and beaches. They are fantastic places for you and your family to explore.

This map shows the locations of a selection of nature reserves where some of the rarest and most beautiful wildflowers in Britain can be found. If you visit any of these special places, record it by placing a tick sticker on this poster.

Go to **www.wildlifetrusts.org** for links to individual Wildlife Trust websites, where you can find detailed maps and information.

THE wildlife TRUSTS

CW00727817

Durham
Hawthorn Dene, Dur
This wooded valley
to many uncommon
including Herb

Early purple orchid

Uplands
Priestcliffe Lees Nature Reserve, Derbyshire WT
You might spot the Early purple orchid in this area of wildflower-rich grassland.

Herb Paris

SCOTLAND

Scotland
Loch Fleet, Scottish WT
Orchids thrive in the heathland of this area, along with this delicate flower.

Twinflower

Bee orchid

Northern Ireland
Slievenacloy Nature Reserve,
Ulster WT

Lincolnshire
Gibraltar Point Nature Reserve, Lincolnshire WT
Sea holly grows on the beaches of this unspoilt stretch of coastline.

Milk parsley

East Anglia
Hickling Broad Nature Reserve, Norfolk WT
Visit this area to see Milk parsley, the only larval food plant of the swallowtail butterfly in the UK.

Frog orchid

Sea holly

Hampshire
St Catherine's Hill Wildlife Reserve, Hampshire & Isle of Wight WT
Look out for the Frog orchid when you're in this area – it's very small and very rare.

NORTHERN IRELAND

Durham

Uplands

Lincolnshire

East Anglia

ENGLAND

Chilterns

WALES

West Country

Hampshire

This vast wildlife paradise is particularly important for orchids.

Yellow horned poppy

Heath lobelia

Wales
Cemlyn Nature Reserve on Angelsey, North Wales WT
Visit this area and you'll see interesting coastal plants such as this poppy.

Chilterns
Warburg Nature Reserve, Berks, Bucks & Oxon WT
In spring, Bluebells carpet the woodlands in this area.

West Country
Andrew's Wood Nature Reserve, Devon WT
Heath lobelia is only found in a few sites in the UK and this area has the largest population.

Bluebell

Copyright © 2010 Miles Kelly Publishing Ltd, Bardfield Centre, Great Bardfield, Essex CM7 4SL, UK

Use the 'SEEN IT!' stickers to record your flower sightings next to their photographs

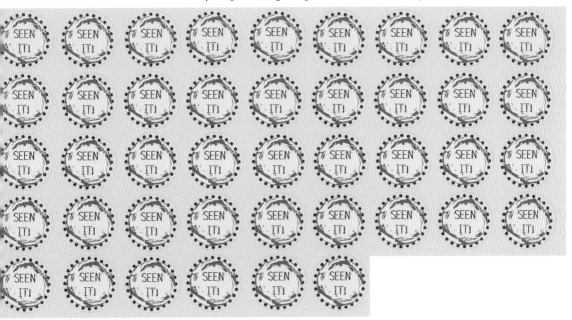

Use the 'LOGGED IT!' stickers when you have recorded your flower sightings at www.wildlifewatch.org.uk

Use the tick stickers on the poster to record your visits to wildflower hotspots

wildflower detectives' handbook

Written by:

Camilla de la Bedoyere

Illustrated by:

Bridgette James

Miles Kelly

First published in 2010 by Miles Kelly Publishing Ltd
Bardfield Centre, Great Bardfield, Essex, CM7 4SL, UK

Copyright © Miles Kelly Publishing Ltd 2010

2 4 6 8 10 9 7 5 3 1

Editorial Director *Belinda Gallagher*
Art Director *Jo Brewer*
Managing Editor *Rosie McGuire*
Assistant Editor *Claire Philip*
Designer *Jo Brewer*
Image Manager *Liberty Newton*
Production Manager *Elizabeth Brunwin*
Reprographics *Stephan Davis, Ian Paulyn*
The Wildlife Trusts Advisor *Adam Cormack*

ISBN 978-1-84810-249-1

Printed in China

British Library Cataloguing-in-Publication Data
A catalogue record for this book is available from the British Library

ACKNOWLEDGEMENTS

The publishers would like to thank Bridgette James for the artwork she contributed to this book. All artworks are by Bridgette James unless otherwise stated. The following artworks are from The Miles Kelly Artwork Bank: Page 5(tr), 7(bl), 17, 53, 85 & 89.

The publishers would like to thank the following sources for the use of their photographs:

Jo Brewer 34 & 54; **dreamstime.com** 12 Elena Elisseeva; 24 Griffin024; 42 Ivonnewierink; 70 Pavel Kalouš; 86 Ryszard; 92 Marcoregalia; **FLPA** Cover & 84 Gary K Smith; 16 FotoNatura/FN/Minden/FLPA; 22 Richard Becker; 50 Erica Olsen; 62 Martin H Smith; 68 Peter Entwistle; 90 Tony Hamblin; 94 Bob Gibbons; **Fotolia.com** Page 6(tr) Elenathewise, (br) Steve Smith; 38 Jgz; 52 Oleg Belyakov; 76 Eric Weight; **Dennis McGuire** 7(tl); 8(tr), (bl); 9(tr); **NHPA** 18 Dr Eckart Pott; 58 Stephen Dalton; **Philip Wells** 36; **The Wildlife Trusts** 20 Rachel Scopes; 14 Neil Aldridge; 26, 28, 40 & 48 Les Binns; 56 & 60 Philip Precey; 66 Eddie Asbery; 80 Dave Appleton; 88 Adam Cormack; Poster (clockwise from top right) **The Wildlife Trusts** Philip Precey; Philip Precey; Lincolnshire Wildlife Trust; David North; Philip Precey; Devon Wildlife Trust; Philip Precey; David North; Neil Aldridge; Scottish Wildlife Trust

All other photographs are from:
Corel, digitalSTOCK, digitalvision, dreamstime.com, Fotolia.com, iStockphoto.com, John Foxx, PhotoAlto, PhotoDisc, PhotoEssentials, PhotoPro, Stockbyte

Contents

Checklist: Mark off your flower sightings in the tick boxes above.

Foreword

Wildflowers are so much more than pretty things that beautify our hedgerows, fields, woods and nature reserves.

They are the foundations on which all ecosystems are built, from the soil in which they grow to the food and shelter they provide for the wild animals that live among their foliage and feed on their leaves, buds, stems and roots. Put names to the wildflowers growing in a certain area and you will start to gain a deeper understanding of every ecosystem you walk through or visit.

This book should help you put a name to a flower. Many widespread species are included, as well as a few that are so spectacular they simply had to make the pages.

Inside, there are over 40 wildflower species to discover. Organised by colour, each species is clearly presented, and there's also space for your photos, sketches and notes. There's even instructions on how to make your own wildflower garden – an opportunity to create a haven for all kinds of wildlife.

Hopefully by using this book you'll start to see wildflowers as part of a bigger picture – the first step towards understanding whole habitats.

What is a flower?

A flower develops inside a bud. Within the petals is a ring of male parts (stamens). Each has a filament topped by an anther containing the male reproductive cells inside pollen grains. At the centre of the flower are the female parts — the stigma and the style. The style widens at its base into an ovary, containing the female reproductive cells in their ovules (eggs).

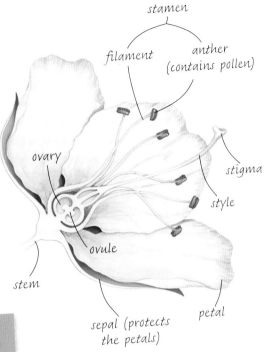

stamen

filament

anther (contains pollen)

ovary

stigma

style

ovule

stem

ovule

sepal (protects the petals)

petal

Pollination: This takes place when an anther releases its pollen, some grains of which travel to the stigma. This allows the male cells in the pollen to reach the female cells in the ovules and fertilise them.

Fruit and seeds: After fertilisation, the ovule turns into a seed and the ovary turns into a fruit. The fruit may become brightly coloured so it is eaten, or dry up and form parachutes or wings to enable it to be blown away.

Glossary

ANNUAL A plant that only lives for one year

BIENNIAL A plant that takes two years to complete its lifecycle

BRACT A scale-like leaf that grows at the bottom of some flower stalks

BULB A swollen part of the plant that grows under the ground, or at ground level. It contains the beginnings of the next year's stems and leaves

FLORET A small flower that is part of a bigger flower head

LEAFLET A leaf can have several parts that look like little leaves, called leaflets

NODE The place where a leaf grows out from a stem

PERENNIAL A plant that lives for more than two years

RACEME A hanging group of flowers

RHIZOME A thickened stem that grows underground or at ground level

ROSETTE The way leaves are arranged around a stem at ground level

SPADIX A flower spike

TENDRIL A thin growth that wraps itself around things

The wildflower calendar

Wildflowers have life-cycles, and these are affected by the changes in the weather that each season brings.

Spring: In spring the soil and air warm up, and the days get longer. Many wildflower plants begin to make an appearance, even if they don't bloom yet.

this is the best season to see wildflowers

look out for green shoots as they sprout from the ground

Summer: Colourful blooms contain sweet nectar that attracts insects to them. The insects will help to fertilise the plant by transferring pollen to the ovaries. Once the tiny ovules inside are fertilised, the ovaries can ripen to form seed cases.

you may see seeds being dispersed

Autumn: Blooms die, but seed cases continue to grow, either drying out or wrapped in soft flesh, such as berries. They may fall to the ground, get eaten or be blown away by the wind. Leaves lose their colour, and fall or wither.

plants that flower early may burst through January snow

Winter: Annual plants die, often when the first frosts bite. Perennial plants rest over winter (they are 'dormant'). There may be no sign of life, but their roots remain alive, underground, waiting for spring.

Become a wildflower detective

All detectives need to prepare before they go exploring, and the same is true for wildflower detectives. Before you set out, check these things:

- Is the weather forecast good? You don't want to get caught in a thunderstorm!
- Have you got your detectives' equipment ready? See the checklist below for a list of things to take.
- Do you know where you are going and how to find your way back?
- Is an adult coming with you?

remember to take photos!

Equipment
Complete the pages in this book with your notes and sketches. Use a ruler to check measurements, and a magnifying glass will give the best view of small plant parts. Take a camera to capture images of entire plants.

Checklist
- O pens
- O pencils
- O rubber
- O ruler
- O camera
- O magnifying glass
- O envelopes/plastic bags (to store samples)
- O sun hat
- O sun cream
- O bottle of water

grass snake

Respect wildlife
Keep dogs under control, close gates after you, take your rubbish home, and don't go on to other people's land without asking their permission. You can pick a sample flower, seed or leaf from most plants, but only take what you need and never pull a plant out of the ground or damage it in any way.

Watch out!
Stinging and biting creatures like wildflowers too. Make sure your feet and legs are covered and use insect repellent on any bare skin.

Make a wildflower garden

Watching nature in action is an amazing experience. If you grow your own wildflowers in the garden you will be treated to glorious colours and scents, as well as plenty of visiting wildlife.

Growing flowers

You can grow flowers from seed, either using seeds you've collected or ones you have bought. The easiest and quickest way to get the garden blooming is to buy plants from garden centres, or online. Small ones are not expensive.

bright colours will attract insects to your garden

- Choose plants that flower at different times, from spring to autumn.
- Sweet-smelling flowers attract moths and bats.
- Purple flowers are the most popular with insects, but if you have a range of colours there will be something for everything.
  - Teasels and sunflowers attract wild birds.
  - Leave ripening seed heads on the flowers, as they are food for animals.
  - Avoid using bug sprays and slug pellets, as garden 'pests' are food for animals such as frogs, newts, lizards, birds and bats.

frogs will eat 'pest' animals such as snails

if you can, leave an area of nettles – butterflies lay their eggs on the leaves

Hiding places

Creatures like to hide, so you will need to leave some parts of the garden undisturbed.

- Make a pile of old wood in a corner, for beetles to bore into
- A patch of ivy is a favourite feeding and resting place for birds, frogs, insects and spiders
- Piles of old leaves will attract shrews and hedgehogs that may nest in them

try leaving a patch of grass to grow long, like a meadow

Give a bee a home

Bees pollinate flowers, which means that their seeds can develop and grow. You can encourage bees into your garden by growing wildflowers and making a bee home.

- Pile up old logs, bricks or a mixture of both and leave plenty of 'tunnel' spaces for bees to crawl into.
- Put plasticine into the bottom of a flowerpot, and push short pieces of old bamboo into it so bees can get into the hollow centres to lay their eggs.
- Put chicken wire into an old flowerpot and add handfuls of dry moss, or small pet bedding for the bees to use as nesting material.
- Use an old birdbox, but put nesting material into it and make the entrance too small for a bird or rat to use.

place bee homes in sheltered places, out of direct sunlight and next to a fence or wall

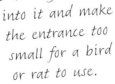

there are about 250 types of bee in Britain

How to use this book

Wildflower detectives like to keep records of what they have seen, and you can do that by filling in the pages of this book. There are spaces for your notes, sketches and photographs.

Seen it?
Once you've seen a species, record it by placing a *Seen It!* sticker.

Photofile
Photos of flower species in their natural habitats, plus extra information.

My observations
Make notes about your sightings and surroundings.

MY OBSERVATIONS

What I can see:

_____
_____
_____
_____

What I can smell:

_____
_____

The weather is:

_____
_____

SEEN IT?

These brightly coloured flowers were sometimes scattered over doorsteps in May. They were also used to remove warts and cure colds.

Drawings: Use a soft pencil, such as 2B, because the lead is easy to rub out. You don't need to draw the whole plant, just the flower, seed case and leaf shape.

MY DRAWINGS AND PHOTOS

My drawings and photos
Fill these spaces with your sketches and photographs.

Photos: Concentrate on taking photos of the whole plant and its habitat. You will need plenty of sunlight, but avoid very bright sunshine because it causes strong black shadows. Make sure your shadow is not cast over the plant.

Logged it?
The flowers in this book are also on the *Wildlife Watch* website (see page 96). Register online to collect nature stars in your profile for spotting these flowers. Once you've logged a sighting, place a *Logged It!* sticker here.

LOGGED IT?

Record your flower sightings at www.wildlifewatch.org.uk

I saw this flower in: March ○   April ○   May ○

86

Main text
Every right-hand page has a main paragraph to introduce you to each species.

Close up
Look here for flower measurements to help you identify each species.

Pressing flowers: If a plant is not marked as poisonous or rare, you might like to press some of its petals. Only take petals from plants that are common. Place the petals between two pieces of thick white paper and slide the paper into a large book. Pile heavy books on top, and leave to dry out for about four weeks. Once the petals are dry, you can stick them into this book.

Marsh marigold Caltha palustris

Marsh marigolds can form large clumps of deep green, shiny leaves, topped by bright golden flowers. The plants are tough and can survive in shady or sunny places, but they prefer damp soil. Marsh marigolds used to be common, but many of their marsh and bog habitats have been lost.

flower is 25 mm across

Colour coding
The flowers in this book are organized by colour. The species pages are coloured to match, making it easy to find your flower.

Illustrations
Detailed artwork shows the key features of each species.

five yellow sepals

TYPE Buttercup family
HEIGHT 20–30 cm
HABITAT Marshes, wet meadows and damp woods
FLOWERS March to July
FRUIT Capsules
OTHER NAMES Kingcup, Mayflower, Water-bubbles

Fact file
This box gives you key information about each species.

Keep safe
You should not touch any part of species that have this symbol on their pages. Other plants may irritate your skin, so it is wise to wash your hands after touching them.

BEWARE! POISONOUS

RARE & PROTECTED

kidney-shaped leaf

strong, upright stem

Rare and protected
You must not take any part of plants that have this symbol on their pages because they are endangered, and you could be breaking the law.

July ○   August ○   September ○   October ○   87

Tick list
Tick to record when you've seen each species in flower.

MY OBSERVATIONS

What I can see:

_____

_____

_____

_____

What I can smell:

_____

_____

The weather is:

_____

_____

Chamomile often grows as a ground covering plant, and is used to create chamomile lawns, which release their scent when walked on.

SEEN IT?

MY DRAWINGS AND PHOTOS

LOGGED IT?

Record your flower sightings at www.wildlifewatch.org.uk

I saw this flower in: March ○   April ○   May ○   June ○

Chamomile *Chamaemelum nobile*

This daisy-like plant is best known for its delicious scent, which is like a mixture of apples and bubblegum. Chamomile used to be widespread, but many of its natural habitats have been destroyed. It is now found growing wild in only a few places in the south of England, especially the New Forest.

flower is about 2 cm across

large yellow disc contains many florets

one flower head on each stalk

petals dip down

TYPE Daisy family

HEIGHT Up to 25 cm

HABITAT Short grassland

FLOWERS June to August

FRUIT Small seeds

OTHER NAMES Roman camomile, Ground apple

grey-green feathery leaves

RARE & PROTECTED

MY OBSERVATIONS

What I can see:

_____

_____

_____

_____

What I can smell:

_____

_____

The weather is:

_____

_____

MY DRAWINGS AND PHOTOS

Meadowsweet keeps blooming through the whole summer, providing food for many insects. Its sweet nectar particularly attracts butterflies and bees.

SEEN IT?

LOGGED IT?

Record your flower sightings at www.wildlifewatch.org.uk

I saw this flower in: March O   April O   May O   June O

Meadowsweet _Filipendula ulmaria_

Meadowsweet has clouds of whitish flowers on tall stems and has a strong perfume. It is popular with flying insects, and thrives in grasslands throughout Britain and Ireland. Long ago, the blooms were scattered over floors to make a house smell sweet.

flower is about 5 mm across

five petals

creamy-white flowers

TYPE Rose family

HEIGHT Up to 125 cm

HABITAT Damp meadows, near streams and marshes

FLOWERS June to September

FRUIT Small, twisted seeds

OTHER NAMES Queen of the meadow, Bridewort

dark green leaves, pale underneath

hairless, reddish stems

July ○   August ○   September ○   October ○

MY OBSERVATIONS

What I can see:

_____

_____

_____

_____

_____

What I can smell:

_____

_____

The weather is:

_____

_____

MY DRAWINGS AND PHOTOS

Fritillary butterflies flock to Oxeye daisies in summer. Their wings have orange-brown markings on the upper surfaces, and paler undersides.

SEEN IT?

I saw this flower in: March O   April O   May O   June O

Oxeye daisy *Leucanthemum vulgare*

Oxeye daisies are common in meadows, where their bright, bold flower heads catch the eye. They grow from year to year, and spread widely to create a carpet of green, topped with white-and-yellow flower heads. Common daisies look similar to these flowers, but they have smooth, oval leaves and only grow to about 10 cm in height.

flower is
3–5 cm across

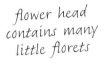

flower head
contains many
little florets

bud

TYPE Daisy family

HEIGHT 10–80 cm

HABITAT Grassy places

FLOWERS May to
September

FRUIT Small seeds

OTHER NAMES Marguerite,
Moon daisy

dark green
leaves with
toothed edge

stalks may be
hairy or smooth

July O   August O   September O   October O

MY OBSERVATIONS

What I can see:

_____

_____

_____

_____

What I can smell:

_____

_____

The weather is:

_____

_____

MY DRAWINGS AND PHOTOS

Water-plantain makes a good resting spot for dragonflies and damselflies. Its roots provide safe hiding places for small fish, beetles and insect larvae.

SEEN IT?

LOGGED IT?

Record your flower sightings at www.wildlifewatch.org.uk

I saw this flower in: March ○   April ○   May ○   June ○

Water-plantain *Alisma plantago-aquatica*

Y ou can see the flowers of this plant best in the afternoon, because they are only open between around 1 pm and 7 pm every day. Water-plantain is a stout plant that grows on the edges of watery habitats, especially ponds. It is found everywhere, except northern Scotland.

flower is
1 cm across

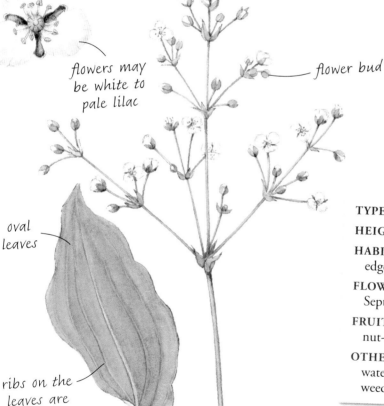

flowers may
be white to
pale lilac

flower bud

oval
leaves

TYPE Water-plantain family

HEIGHT Up to 100 cm

HABITAT Shallow water,
edges of lakes and ponds

FLOWERS June to
September

FRUIT Green, small and
nut-like

OTHER NAMES Common
water-plantain, Mad-dog
weed

ribs on the
leaves are
curved

long stalks
on each leaf

stem

July O   August O   September O   October O

MY OBSERVATIONS

What I can see:

_____

_____

_____

_____

_____

What I can smell:

_____

_____

The weather is:

_____

_____

Wood anemones are found in the same habitats as Bluebells, which also come into flower during spring. Look out for them together, as they look beautiful on a woodland floor.

SEEN IT?

MY DRAWINGS AND PHOTOS

LOGGED IT?

Record your flower sightings at www.wildlifewatch.org.uk

I saw this flower in: March ○   April ○   May ○   June ○

Wood anemone Anemone nemorosa

Wood anemones come into flower in spring, so they decorate woodland floors before many trees have unfurled their leaves. These flowers are able to move towards the light, so they follow the sun as it moves through the sky. Although they have a slight scent, Wood anemones do not contain nectar, so insects visiting the flowers may leave hungry.

flower is about 2.5 cm across

each flower has five to ten petals

each leaf has three lobes

long stalks on leaves

petals (which are actually sepals) have a pinkish hue

TYPE Buttercup family

HEIGHT Up to 30 cm

HABITAT Woodlands, hedgerows and meadows

FLOWERS March and April

FRUIT Clusters of seeds on old flower head

OTHER NAMES Windflower, Thimbleweed

BEWARE! POISONOUS

July O   August O   September O   October O

MY OBSERVATIONS

What I can see:

_____

_____

_____

_____

_____

What I can smell:

_____

_____

The weather is:

_____

_____

Red helleborines usually grow in shady places. These wild flowers are extremely rare, and are found in only a few places in southern England.

SEEN IT?

MY DRAWINGS AND PHOTOS

LOGGED IT?

Record your flower sightings at www.wildlifewatch.org.uk

22   I saw this flower in: March ○   April ○   May ○   June ○

Broad-leaved helleborine *Epipactis helleborine*

The Broad-leaved helleborine is a striking plant, with a single spike that grows tall, bearing up to 100 flowers. Its delicately coloured petals are similar to those of other orchids, and are perfectly shaped to put pollen on the back of any visiting bees. Look out for wasps feeding on the nectar, or ants climbing into the cup-shaped flowers.

flower is
2 cm across

sepals look
like petals

tall flower
spike

flowers are pale,
but with purple edges

large, oval-
shaped leaves
with veins

TYPE Orchid family

HEIGHT Up to 90 cm

HABITAT Woodlands,
verges, limestone cliffs

FLOWERS July to
September

FRUIT Pear-shaped

OTHER NAMES None

stem has
soft hairs

roots at ground level

July ○   August ○   September ○   October ○

MY OBSERVATIONS

What I can see:

_____

_____

_____

_____

What I can smell:

_____

_____

The weather is:

_____

_____

MY DRAWINGS AND PHOTOS

If the spathe is cut open the flowers can be seen growing on the spadix. The female flowers are at the base and darker male flowers grow just above them.

SEEN IT?

— spadix

male flowers

female flowers

I saw this flower in: March ○   April ○   May ○   June ○

Lords and ladies *Arum maculatum*

The flowers from a Lords and ladies plant produce a strong, unpleasant smell that attracts insects, which crawl into the flower heads looking for nectar. As they search, the insects rub against the pollen in the male flowers, and fertilise the female ones. Insects may get trapped and die, and their bodies can be seen in the spathe.

spadix is 5 cm tall

thick leaf, called a spathe, which protects the growing flower

flower-bearing stalk, called the spadix

red berries

large, arrow-shaped leaves

stiff, upright stem

TYPE Arum family

HEIGHT Up to 50 cm

HABITAT Woodlands and hedgerows

FLOWERS April and May

FRUIT Red berries

OTHER NAMES Cuckoo pint, Sweethearts, Adam and Eve

BEWARE! POISONOUS

July O   August O   September O   October O   25

MY OBSERVATIONS

What I can see:

_____

_____

_____

_____

What I can smell:

_____

_____

The weather is:

_____

_____

The lower petal of this orchid looks like a bee. Male bees are attracted to it, and as they settle on the flower their backs are coated in pollen.

SEEN IT?

MY DRAWINGS AND PHOTOS

I saw this flower in: March ○   April ○   May ○   June ○

Bee orchid *Orphrys apifera*

There are around 40 members of the wild orchid family in England and Wales, and Bee orchids are one of the best known and most widespread of them. Each stem holds between two and seven flowers, and each flower looks as if a fat bumblebee has settled on it. Bee orchids are probably extinct in Scotland.

flower is 4 cm top to bottom

bud

upper petals are rolled, like cylinders, often green or brown

central lobe of lower petal feels like velvet

TYPE Orchid family

HEIGHT Up to 30 cm

HABITAT Dry grasslands, especially near chalky or limestone areas

FLOWERS June and July

FRUIT Long and green with ridges

OTHER NAMES None

leaves are pointed and slender

leafy stem

July ○   August ○   September ○   October ○   27

MY OBSERVATIONS

What I can see:

_____

_____

_____

_____

What I can smell:

_____

_____

The weather is:

_____

_____

Heathers such as the cross-leaved heath tend to keep their leaves over the winter. Their flowers are usually small and bell-like.

SEEN IT?

MY DRAWINGS AND PHOTOS

LOGGED IT?

Record your flower sightings at www.wildlifewatch.org.uk

I saw this flower in: March ○   April ○   May ○   June ○

Cross-leaved heath *Erica tetralix*

This evergreen plant keeps its leaves all year round. They are arranged in a circle, called a whorl, around the stem. Cross-leaved heath has pretty pink flowers, which hang like bells. They stay on the plant until late summer, making a colourful display in boggy places, and attract bees.

flower is
6 mm long

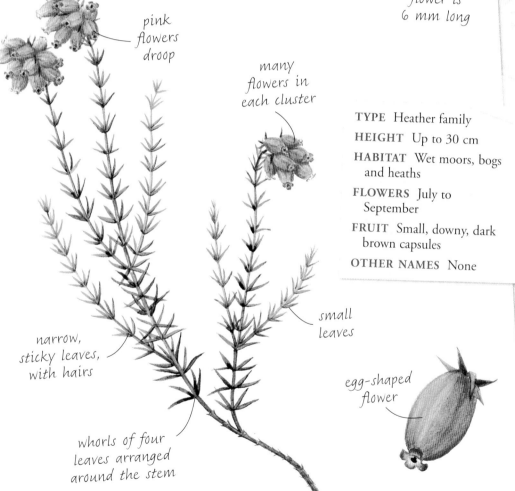

pink
flowers
droop

many
flowers in
each cluster

TYPE Heather family

HEIGHT Up to 30 cm

HABITAT Wet moors, bogs and heaths

FLOWERS July to September

FRUIT Small, downy, dark brown capsules

OTHER NAMES None

small
leaves

narrow,
sticky leaves,
with hairs

egg-shaped
flower

whorls of four
leaves arranged
around the stem

July O   August O   September O   October O

MY OBSERVATIONS

What I can see:

_____

_____

_____

_____

What I can smell:

_____

_____

The weather is:

_____

_____

Sweet williams, shown here, are related to Deptford pinks, and are popular in gardens. Their flowers are larger than those of Deptford pinks, and grow in a range of colours.

SEEN IT?

MY DRAWINGS AND PHOTOS

I saw this flower in: March ○   April ○   May ○   June ○

Deptford pink *Dianthus armeria*

The colour of this flower's petals is often described as cerise, and its stem is greyish. Deptford pinks are biennial, which means that their life-cycle takes two years. This plant produces up to 400 seeds at the end of the summer. A round clump, or rosette, of leaves grows the following year, and flowers bloom the year after that.

flower is up to 15 mm wide

flowers grow at top of stems

five petals

thin leaves, with hairs

straight, slender stem

TYPE Pink family

HEIGHT Up to 60 cm

HABITAT Dry, grassy areas

FLOWERS June to August

FRUIT Small capsules

OTHER NAMES Mountain pink

RARE & PROTECTED

MY OBSERVATIONS

What I can see:

_____

_____

_____

_____

What I can smell:

_____

_____

The weather is:

_____

_____

MY DRAWINGS AND PHOTOS

As bees crawl into a Foxglove flower they get covered in pollen. They transfer pollen to other flowers. In doing so they fertilise the eggs, which then grow into seeds.

SEEN IT?

I saw this flower in: March ○   April ○   May ○   June ○

Foxglove *Digitalis purpurea*

This flower is easy to spot, with its tall spikes that are covered in up to 80 pink flowers. The plant gets its name from the tube-shaped flowers, which are said to resemble little gloves for a fox. The large, pale green leaves are soft on top and woolly underneath.

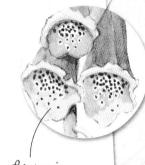

flower is 4 cm long

seed case

raceme (flower spike) with 20 to 80 flowers on it

pink-purple flowers

TYPE Digitalis family

HEIGHT 40–150 cm

HABITAT Woodlands, moors, open spaces, heaths

FLOWERS June to August

FRUIT Green capsules

OTHER NAMES Dead mans' bells, Witches' gloves

inside the flower there is a white part, purple spots and hairs

woolly stem and leaves

BEWARE! POISONOUS

MY OBSERVATIONS

What I can see:

_____

_____

_____

_____

_____

What I can smell:

_____

_____

The weather is:

_____

_____

MY DRAWINGS AND PHOTOS

These flowers are called codlins-and-cream because they are pink and white. Codlins were rosy apples that were boiled in milk and served with cream.

SEEN IT?

Great willowherb *Epilobium hirsutum*

Willowherbs are unusually tall wildflowers, so it is easy to find them in damp places throughout Britain, except the far north-west, where they rarely grow. They can come from seeds, but they also spread out by fattened roots, called rhizomes, in the soil. This can lead to a large, colourful clump forming in one spot.

flower is 25 mm across

flowerless stalk

rosy-pink petals attract bees and hoverflies

TYPE Willowherb family

HEIGHT Up to 200 cm

HABITAT Damp places, such as fens, riverbanks and ditches

FLOWERS July and August

FRUIT Soft pods contain airborne seeds

OTHER NAMES Hairy willowherb, Codlins-and-cream

long, narrow leaves, pointed

creamy-white stigma

woolly stems and leaves

July O   August O   September O   October O

MY OBSERVATIONS

What I can see:

_____
_____
_____
_____

What I can smell:

_____
_____

The weather is:

_____
_____

Heather was once used as bedding for animals and bound to make rope, brooms and thatch for roofs. It was even used to repair holes in roads and burnt as a fuel.

SEEN IT?

MY DRAWINGS AND PHOTOS

I saw this flower in: March O   April O   May O   June O

Heather *Calluna vulgaris*

You can find Heather in both damp and dry places. It grows into bushes with many branches and each bush can reach 100 cm tall and 100 cm wide. Heather keeps its leaves over the winter, and its flowers, which are sometimes white, can last from spring to autumn.

flower is 4 mm across

flowers grow from narrow spikes

bell-shaped flower

leaves grow in rows

woody stem

TYPE Heather family

HEIGHT 50–100 cm

HABITAT Heaths, moors, bogs, open spaces and woods

FLOWERS July to September

FRUIT Capsules

OTHER NAMES Common heather, Ling

July ○   August ○   September ○   October ○

MY OBSERVATIONS

What I can see:

_____

_____

_____

_____

_____

What I can smell:

_____

_____

The weather is:

_____

_____

Herb-Robert turns red in the autumn. Although it is very pretty, this plant can quickly take over an area, killing off weaker plants that cannot reach the light.

SEEN IT?

MY DRAWINGS AND PHOTOS

LOGGED IT?

Record your flower sightings at www.wildlifewatch.org.uk

I saw this flower in: March O   April O   May O   June O

Herb-Robert _Geranium robertianum_

Herb-Robert is a survivor. It can live in sun or shade, and can cope with mild winter weather, unlike many other wildflowers that die down after the summer. As Herb-Robert is not fussy about the type of soil it lives in, it is common throughout Britain.

five petals
on a flower

petals can be
pink or white

seed case

flower is
12 mm across

feathery leaves

red stems,
hairy and oily

TYPE Crane's-bill family

HEIGHT 10–50 cm

HABITAT Hedgerows, near
shady walls, pathways,
woods

FLOWERS April to October

FRUIT Long and hairy

OTHER NAMES Red robin,
Stinky-Bob

July O August O September O October O

MY OBSERVATIONS

What I can see:

_____

_____

_____

_____

What I can smell:

_____

_____

The weather is:

_____

_____

In some places, Indian balsam is called 'bee-bums', because when a bee is exploring inside the flower, feeding on nectar, all you can see is its tail end!

SEEN IT?

MY DRAWINGS AND PHOTOS

LOGGED IT?

Record your flower sightings at www.wildlifewatch.org.uk

I saw this flower in: March ○   April ○   May ○   June ○

Indian balsam _Impatiens glandulifera_

Indian balsam was introduced to Britain in 1839, having been brought from the Himalayan mountain region. It is one of the tallest wildflowers, and is seen all over Britain, especially in England and Wales. The flowers produce lots of nectar, so there are likely to be bees, wasps and other insects nearby.

flower is
3 cm across

petals are pink
or occasionally
white

orchid-like
flowers

TYPE Often treated as a weed

HEIGHT 100–200 cm

HABITAT Wet places, near rivers and streams

FLOWERS July to October

FRUIT Explosive seed pods

OTHER NAMES Policeman's balsam, Kiss-me-on-the-mountain

slender leaves
with toothed
edges

reddish
stems

explosive
seed pod

July O   August O   September O   October O

MY OBSERVATIONS

What I can see:

_____

_____

_____

_____

_____

What I can smell:

_____

_____

The weather is:

_____

_____

Clumps of Purple-loosestrife attract many types of wildlife, including bumblebees, honeybees, brimstone butterflies and elephant hawk-moths.

SEEN IT?

MY DRAWINGS AND PHOTOS

LOGGED IT?

Record your flower sightings at www.wildlifewatch.org.uk

I saw this flower in: March O   April O   May O   June O

Purple-loosestrife Lythrum salicaria

Purple-loosestrife plants often grow close together in wet places, with their magenta-pink flower spikes standing tall above the green leaves. These plants are perennial, which means they can live for more than two years before dying down, and the flowers last for the whole summer.

flower is
15 mm across

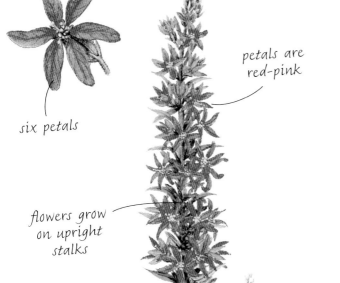

petals are
red-pink

six petals

flowers grow
on upright
stalks

long, slender
leaves grow in pairs,
opposite each other

TYPE Wetland plant that grows in groups

HEIGHT Up to 200 cm

HABITAT Wetlands, near pond edges, marshes and fens

FLOWERS June to August

FRUIT Capsule containing tiny seeds

OTHER NAMES None

July O   August O   September O   October O   43

MY OBSERVATIONS

What I can see:

_____

_____

_____

_____

_____

What I can smell:

_____

_____

The weather is:

_____

_____

MY DRAWINGS AND PHOTOS

Red campion blooms as Bluebells are finishing. Woodlands with Wood anemones, Bluebells and Red campion go through shades of white, blue and pink from spring to autumn.

SEEN IT?

LOGGED IT?

Record your flower sightings at www.wildlifewatch.org.uk

I saw this flower in: March O   April O   May O   June O

Red campion *Silene dioica*

The flowers of Red campion are mostly pink rather than red. There are five petals on each flower head, but it can look as if there are more when the petals are very deeply lobed. The flowers are visited by bumblebees, butterflies and moths, which feed on the sweet nectar.

flower is up to 25 mm across

pink petals, occasionally with red tips

TYPE Pink family

HEIGHT Up to 100 cm

HABITAT Hedgerows, paths, grassy places

FLOWERS March to October

FRUIT Round, dry capsule

OTHER NAMES Adders' flower, Jack-by-the-hedge, Scalded apples

long, hairy stems, slightly sticky

seed capsule

oval hairy leaves in pairs

MY OBSERVATIONS

What I can see:

_____

_____

_____

_____

What I can smell:

_____

_____

The weather is:

_____

According to folklore, if you have Thrift in your garden you will never be poor. Named after the practice of taking care of your money, it was depicted on the back of an old English coin.

SEEN IT?

MY DRAWINGS AND PHOTOS

LOGGED IT?

Record your flower sightings at www.wildlifewatch.org.uk

I saw this flower in: March ○   April ○   May ○   June ○

Thrift *Armeria maritima*

Thrift has candyfloss flower heads growing above a dense mat of leaves. It is an unusual plant that can grow in very dry places, especially at the coast. The clump of leaves makes a safe home for beetles and other insects, and bees visit the pink flowers. When many clumps grow together, they create a cushion of soft leaves.

flower head is 2 cm across

round flower heads with lots of little flowers

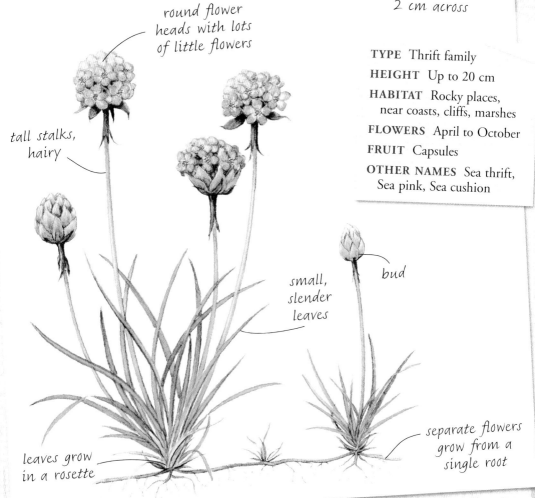

tall stalks, hairy

TYPE Thrift family
HEIGHT Up to 20 cm
HABITAT Rocky places, near coasts, cliffs, marshes
FLOWERS April to October
FRUIT Capsules
OTHER NAMES Sea thrift, Sea pink, Sea cushion

small, slender leaves

bud

leaves grow in a rosette

separate flowers grow from a single root

MY OBSERVATIONS

What I can see:

_____

_____

_____

_____

_____

What I can smell:

_____

_____

The weather is:

_____

_____

Although the flower of this plant is very distinctive, you can still recognise it when it is not in bloom by its large, toothed leaves, which are mostly divided into five leaflets.

SEEN IT?

MY DRAWINGS AND PHOTOS

LOGGED IT?

Record your flower sightings at www.wildlifewatch.org.uk

I saw this flower in: March O   April O   May O   June O

Marsh cinquefoil _Potentilla palustris_

The deep pink or red flowers of the Marsh cinquefoil are unlike any other flower. They are star shaped, and grow at the top of upright magenta-coloured stems. There are five sepals and smaller purple petals form a layer on top of them. Other cinquefoils, which grow in dry places, have yellow flowers and are not star shaped.

flower is 2 cm across

petals

sepals

upper leaves may have just three leaflets

lowest leaves may have five leaflets

TYPE Rose family

HEIGHT 20–50 cm

HABITAT Wet places, fens, marshes, bogs and near ponds

FLOWERS June and July

FRUIT Dry, small and papery

OTHER NAMES Swamp cinquefoil

July ○   August ○   September ○   October ○

49

MY OBSERVATIONS

What I can see:

_____

_____

_____

_____

_____

What I can smell:

_____

_____

The weather is:

_____

_____

This flower is rare, as each plant only produces a few heavy seeds that are not easily transported to new areas. It has also been killed off in many areas by the use of chemicals.

SEEN IT?

MY DRAWINGS AND PHOTOS

LOGGED IT?

Record your flower sightings at www.wildlifewatch.org.uk

I saw this flower in: March ○   April ○   May ○   June ○

Pheasant's eye *Adonis annua*

flower is
3 cm across

Pheasant's eye is a type of buttercup, with five to eight glossy scarlet petals and feathery leaves. By August the flowers are dying down to be replaced by large seed cases. When the seeds fall to the ground they may rest there – they are described as 'dormant' – until the following spring, or even several years later.

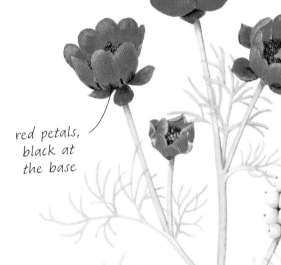

black centre

red petals,
black at
the base

large seed
case

feathery,
delicate leaves

TYPE Buttercup family

HEIGHT Up to 40 cm

HABITAT Farmers' fields

FLOWERS June to August

FRUIT Large and wrinkled

OTHER NAMES Blood drops, Jack in the green, Rose-a-ruby

RARE & PROTECTED

MY OBSERVATIONS

What I can see:

_____

_____

_____

_____

What I can smell:

_____

_____

The weather is:

_____

_____

Poppies are common in farmers' fields because they grow particularly well on soil that has been disturbed, and they can flower and seed themselves before the farmer's crop is harvested.

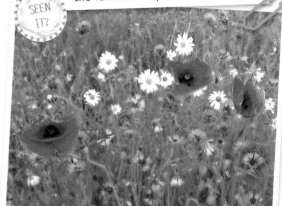

SEEN IT?

MY DRAWINGS AND PHOTOS

Record your flower sightings at www.wildlifewatch.org.uk

I saw this flower in: March ○   April ○   May ○   June ○

Poppy *Papaver rhoeas*

The scarlet, papery petals of the Poppy are often black at the base. The flowers grow at the top of a long, hairy stalk and each petal is black at the base. The leaves are distinctive, with their feathery appearance and toothed edges.

flower is
7 cm across

four
petals

seed head
droops

hairy
stalks

long slender leaves,
divided to give a
feathery appearance

TYPE Poppy family

HEIGHT 40–80 cm

HABITAT Fields, wasteland, roadsides

FLOWERS June to August

FRUIT Round capsule

OTHER NAMES Common poppy, Flanders poppy, Corn poppy

tough seed
case

MY OBSERVATIONS

What I can see:

_____

_____

_____

_____

What I can smell:

_____

_____

The weather is:

_____

_____

The petals of Scarlet pimpernel close when air pressure drops – a sign that rain might be due. It can also be used to tell the time, as petals open in the morning and close mid-afternoon.

SEEN IT?

MY DRAWINGS AND PHOTOS

Scarlet pimpernel *Anagalis arvensis*

*I*t is easy to overlook the tiny red flowers of the Scarlet pimpernel. These plants are small and grow low to the ground, with the stems sprawling out along the soil. Purple hairs inside the flower attract many insects in summer. Scarlet pimpernels are common throughout Britain, but are mostly found near the coast in Scotland.

flower is
12 mm across

bright scarlet
flowers

egg-shaped
leaves

creeping stems

black dots on
underside of leaves

TYPE Primrose family

HEIGHT Up to 20 cm

HABITAT Farms, grassland, open areas and sand dunes

FLOWERS May to September

FRUIT Tiny brown capsules

OTHER NAMES Red chickweed, Red pimpernel, Shepherd's clock

MY OBSERVATIONS

What I can see:

_____

_____

_____

_____

What I can smell:

_____

_____

The weather is:

_____

_____

Beautiful Bluebells carpet woodland floors in spring, creating a stunning sight. Visitors like to enjoy the floral display and strong fragrance.

SEEN IT?

MY DRAWINGS AND PHOTOS

LOGGED IT?

Record your flower sightings at www.wildlifewatch.org.uk

I saw this flower in: March ○   April ○   May ○   June ○

Bluebell *Hyacinthoides non-scripta*

These plants normally bear blue flowers, but there are violet, pink and white ones too. Flower spikes grow from a clump of deep green leaves. Each spike bears four to 16 bell-shaped flowers in clusters. Bluebells were once common, but many Bluebell woods have been damaged by people picking the flowers and digging up the bulbs.

flower is
15 mm long

papery
seed case

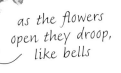

flower spikes
(racemes) are upright
when in bud

as the flowers
open they droop,
like bells

TYPE Lily family

HEIGHT 10–40 cm

HABITAT Woodlands and
coastal cliffs

FLOWERS April to June

FRUIT Capsules

OTHER NAMES Wood bells,
Auld man's bell, Jacinth,
Ring o' bells

strong, long
and glossy
leaves

RARE &
PROTECTED

July ○   August ○   September ○   October ○   57

MY OBSERVATIONS

What I can see:

_____

_____

_____

_____

_____

What I can smell:

_____

_____

The weather is:

_____

_____

MY DRAWINGS AND PHOTOS

Brooklime grows in wet ground and in water. Its leaves and stems provide shelter for small pond-living animals such as insects, sticklebacks (small fish) and tadpoles.

SEEN IT?

LOGGED IT?

Record your flower sightings at www.wildlifewatch.org.uk

I saw this flower in: March O   April O   May O   June O

Brooklime *Veronica beccabunga*

Brooklime is a creeping plant that produces stems that grow along the ground. Roots grow from these stems at places called nodes. The flowering stems grow upright and produce star-shaped blooms throughout the summer. The petals are usually blue, but pink ones grow too, and there is a white 'eye' in the centre of each bloom.

flower is
3 cm across

four
petals

small blue
flowers

oval, fleshy
leaves

creeping
stems

root

node

TYPE Water plant of the Speedwell family

HEIGHT Up to 30 cm

HABITAT Any damp ground, often grows in shallow water

FLOWERS May to September

FRUIT Round flat capsules

OTHER NAMES Water pimpernel, Cow cress, Limewort

July O   August O   September O   October O

MY OBSERVATIONS

What I can see:

_____

_____

_____

_____

What I can smell:

_____

_____

The weather is:

_____

_____

MY DRAWINGS AND PHOTOS

This plant grows throughout Britain. In some places it is called Carpenter's herb, because it was once used to stop bleeding and people often grew it in their gardens for that purpose.

SEEN IT?

Bugle *Ajuga reptans*

Bugle forms dense mats of green leaves, covering the ground. Flower stems grow upwards and bear clusters of many small, purple flowers. Occasionally, the flowers are pink or white. Bugle leaves are unusual because they have a dark green background colour, with a purple sheen. Butterflies often flitter around this plant and feed on it.

flower is
15 mm long

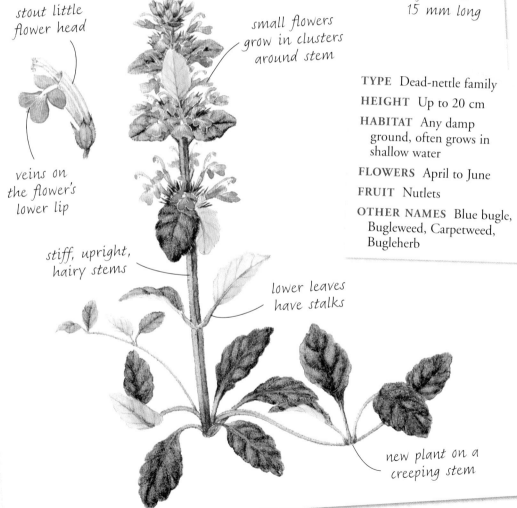

stout little
flower head

small flowers
grow in clusters
around stem

veins on
the flower's
lower lip

stiff, upright,
hairy stems

lower leaves
have stalks

new plant on a
creeping stem

TYPE Dead-nettle family

HEIGHT Up to 20 cm

HABITAT Any damp
ground, often grows in
shallow water

FLOWERS April to June

FRUIT Nutlets

OTHER NAMES Blue bugle,
Bugleweed, Carpetweed,
Bugleherb

MY OBSERVATIONS

What I can see: _____

_____

_____

_____

_____

What I can smell: _____

_____

The weather is: _____

_____

Butterworts are pretty insect-eaters. Flowers grow from single stems, which emerge out of a single rosette of leaves at ground level.

SEEN IT?

MY DRAWINGS AND PHOTOS

I saw this flower in: March ○   April ○   May ○   June ○

Butterwort *Pinguicula vulgaris*

These violet flowers attract bees, to pollinate them. A sticky leaf attracts flies and other small insects, holding them like glue and stopping them from breathing. The leaves then curl around the bugs and produce chemicals that start to dissolve their bodies. This releases nutrients that help the plant to grow.

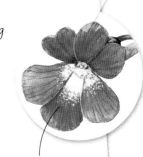

flower is
12 mm across

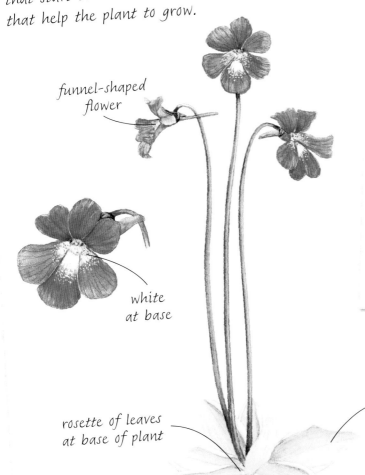

funnel-shaped
flower

white
at base

TYPE Fly-eating plant

HEIGHT Up to 15 cm

HABITAT Bogs and other damp places

FLOWERS May to August

FRUIT Tough, oval-shaped capsule

OTHER NAMES None

yellow-green
leaves, sticky

rosette of leaves
at base of plant

MY OBSERVATIONS

What I can see:

_____

_____

_____

_____

What I can smell:

_____

_____

The weather is:

_____

_____

Columbine is poisonous but it was once used to treat digestive problems, and as a painkiller. It was also thought that carrying a posy of Columbine would make people fall in love.

SEEN IT?

MY DRAWINGS AND PHOTOS

Columbine _Aquilegia vulgaris_

Columbine flowers grow on tall stems. The central part of the flower is made up of five petals, and a rosette of coloured leaves surrounds them, to create a drooping, stunning bloom. Wild Columbines are deep blue to purple in colour and have a fragrance.

flower is
35 mm long

nodding
purple-blue
flower

TYPE Buttercup family

HEIGHT Up to 100 cm

HABITAT Open woods, fens and grasslands

FLOWERS May to August

FRUIT Small and dry but with many seeds

OTHER NAMES None

grey-green
leaves, divided

leafless
stem

leaves grow
as a clump at
the ground

BEWARE!
POISONOUS

July ○   August ○   September ○   October ○

MY OBSERVATIONS

What I can see:
_____
_____
_____
_____

What I can smell:
_____
_____

The weather is:
_____

MY DRAWINGS AND PHOTOS

Cornflowers were used in herbal medicine to treat eye problems, and young men in love often wore them in their buttonholes.

SEEN IT?

Cornflower *Centaurea cyanus*

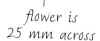

Cornflower blooms are such a brilliant blue that they have given their name to a shade of the colour. Each bloom is actually a collection of tiny flowers, called florets. The outer florets are blue to purple, and the inner florets are slightly redder. Cornflowers were once common in farmers' fields, but are now a rare sight.

flower is 25 mm across

inner floret

tufted flower heads

outer floret

stem is swollen just below the flower head

narrow leaves, grey-green

leaves grow alternately up the stem

TYPE Daisy family

HEIGHT 40–90 cm

HABITAT Fields

FLOWERS June to August

FRUIT Small

OTHER NAMES Bachelor's button, Bluebottle, Basketflower

RARE & PROTECTED

July O   August O   September O   October O

MY OBSERVATIONS

What I can see:

_____

_____

_____

_____

_____

What I can smell:

_____

_____

The weather is:

_____

_____

Insects, such as this butterfly, are attracted to these flowers because they suck the sugary nectar that the flowers produce. In return, the insects pollinate the plants.

SEEN IT?

MY DRAWINGS AND PHOTOS

Devil's-bit scabious *Succisa pratensis*

The round bloom of a Devil's-bit scabious is not one flower, but many little florets all clustered together. The petals are usually purple-blue, but are sometimes pinkish. The tiny anthers in each flower poke out above the petals. Bumblebees are drawn to the flowers because they prefer purple blooms to those of any other colour.

flower is 2 cm across

domed flower head

stems may be hairy

upright stem

leaves mostly grow near bottom of stem

TYPE Teasel family

HEIGHT 10–75 cm

HABITAT Damp grasslands, open areas, hedgerows, mountain slopes

FLOWERS June to September

FRUIT Dry and papery

OTHER NAMES Pincushion flowers

July ○   August ○   September ○   October ○

MY OBSERVATIONS

What I can see:

_____

_____

_____

_____

What I can smell:

_____

_____

The weather is:

_____

_____

Harebells can live from year to year because they grow rhizomes. In the autumn, the plants die down but the rhizomes are safe in the ground, and produce new stems in the spring.

SEEN IT?

MY DRAWINGS AND PHOTOS

Harebell *Campanula rotundifolia*

The flowers of the Harebell are delicate and swing when a breeze catches them. Each stem may bear just one flower, or several growing on a spike. The leaves grow long and thin near the flowers, but round when they are near the base. At ground level, creeping stems become thick and store food over winter for the plant.

flower is 15 mm long

blue petals, occasionally white

hanging flowers

TYPE Harebell family

HEIGHT 10–40 cm

HABITAT Dry grasslands, dunes, hedges and heaths

FLOWERS July to October

FRUIT Dry capsules

OTHER NAMES Bluebell, Witches' thimbles, Fairy bells, Old man's bells

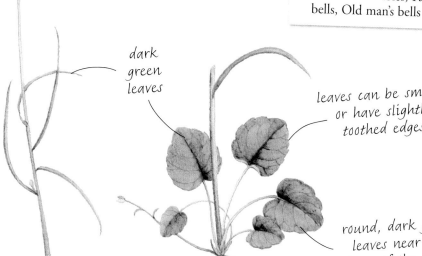

dark green leaves

leaves can be smooth or have slightly toothed edges

round, dark green leaves near the base of the stem

July O   August O   September O   October O

MY OBSERVATIONS

What I can see:

_____

_____

_____

_____

_____

What I can smell:

_____

_____

The weather is:

_____

Wild pansies are also part of the violet family and they grow in dry grasslands and gardens. Their flowers can be violet, yellow or a combination of the two.

SEEN IT?

MY DRAWINGS AND PHOTOS

Marsh violet *Viola palustris*

Violets look like pansies, but are a little smaller. Marsh violet flowers are pale lilac or violet in colour and the lower petal has deep purple veins. After the flower dies the petals fall off, but the five sepals stay attached to the stalk and the growing seed capsule. The caterpillars of fritillary butterflies use this as a food plant.

flower is 12 mm across

stalks droop at the top

four upright petals

long stalks

lower petal is large and lobed

TYPE Violet family

HEIGHT 5–20 cm

HABITAT Bogs, marshes, riverbanks and damp meadows

FLOWERS April to July

FRUIT Egg-shaped

OTHER NAMES Alpine marsh violet

leaves are kidney shaped or round

MY OBSERVATIONS

What I can see:

_____

_____

_____

_____

What I can smell:

_____

_____

The weather is:

_____

Crane's bills are also called geraniums. They can survive from year to year, and grow in bigger and bigger mounds. Most geraniums are blue, violet, purple or pink.

SEEN IT?

MY DRAWINGS AND PHOTOS

LOGGED IT?

Record your flower sightings at www.wildlifewatch.org.uk

74

I saw this flower in: March ○   April ○   May ○   June ○

Meadow crane's bill *Geranium pratense*

flower is
3 cm across

The purple-blue flowers of the Meadow crane's bill grow tall above the surface of a clump of dark green leaves, providing a summer splash of colour. These flowers grow all over Britain but look similar to Wood crane's bill, which is paler in colour, but is only found in the north of England and Scotland.

flowers grow
in pairs

five petals

fruit has a
long beak

hairy
stems

large jagged
leaves, round

TYPE Crane's bill family

HEIGHT 20–80 cm

HABITAT Meadows, woods, grasslands, dunes and roadsides

FLOWERS June to September

FRUIT Small but with a long 'beak'

OTHER NAMES None

July ○   August ○   September ○   October ○

MY OBSERVATIONS

What I can see:

_____

_____

_____

_____

What I can smell:

_____

_____

The weather is:

_____

MY DRAWINGS AND PHOTOS

Teasels are especially popular with goldfinches. These bold, noisy, colourful birds flock to the dry heads to feast on the seeds inside. A group of goldfinches is called a charm.

SEEN IT?

Teasel *Dipascus fullonum*

Teasel plants produce flowers only in their second year. In the first year, the plant grows a large rosette of leaves at ground level. In the second year, a large stem grows from the rosette to hold the flower head. The rosette then dies back and paired prickly leaves grow on the flower stem.

large flower head with purple flowers

flower is 7 cm long

prickly leaves and flower stem

TYPE Teasel family

HEIGHT Up to 200 cm

HABITAT Grasslands, near streams, roadsides, wasteland and by railways

FLOWERS July and August

FRUIT Dry flower heads hold many dry fruits

OTHER NAMES Wild teasel, Brushes-and-combs

leaves have no stalks and grow in pairs

MY OBSERVATIONS

What I can see:

_____

_____

_____

_____

_____

What I can smell:

_____

_____

The weather is:

_____

_____

Tufted vetch is also known as Cow vetch because it can be fed to cattle. It grows in wild woodlands where deer may roam. Like other pea plants, it adds goodness to the soil.

SEEN IT?

MY DRAWINGS AND PHOTOS

LOGGED IT?

Record your flower sightings at www.wildlifewatch.org.uk

I saw this flower in: March ○   April ○   May ○   June ○

Tufted vetch *Vicia cracca*

Like other members of the pea family, Tufted vetch has many oval leaflets that are paired on one stalk. Curling tendrils grow from the end of some leaflets. They help pea plants to climb and clamber high, catching the sun and blocking the light from other plants. The blue-purple flowers grow in clusters where leaflets connect to the stem.

flower is
1 cm long

clusters of
flowers on
a raceme

TYPE Pea family

HEIGHT 30–200 cm

HABITAT Grassy places, hedgerows, bushes and ditches

FLOWERS June to August

FRUIT Bright green pods

OTHER NAMES Cow vetch

branched
tendril

up to 12 pairs of
leaflets on one stalk,
pairs are not exactly
opposite

long pods,
hairy

blue-purple
flower

July O   August O   September O   October O

MY OBSERVATIONS

What I can see:

_____

_____

_____

_____

What I can smell:

_____

_____

The weather is:

_____

_____

Cowslips have long been used in traditional medicine to treat coughs and headaches. They can also be made into wine, or used to add flavour and colour to recipes.

SEEN IT?

MY DRAWINGS AND PHOTOS

LOGGED IT?

Record your flower sightings at www.wildlifewatch.org.uk

I saw this flower in: March ○   April ○   May ○   June ○

Cowslip *Primula veris*

Cowslips have rosettes of large, wrinkled leaves at the base and clusters of yellow flowers that are held high on tall stems. They were once widespread, but became less common in recent years. Today, hedgerows and meadows are often left uncut until autumn, so flowers like these have a better chance of surviving.

flower is
12 mm across

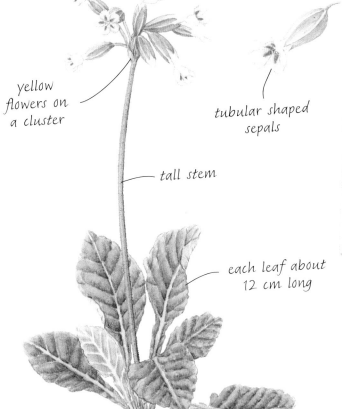

yellow
flowers on
a cluster

tubular shaped
sepals

tall stem

TYPE Primrose family

HEIGHT 10–30 cm

HABITAT Grassy places, open woods, meadows and roadsides

FLOWERS April and May

FRUIT Capsules

OTHER NAMES Herb-Peter

each leaf about
12 cm long

thick, wrinkly
leaves in a rosette

July ○　　　August ○　　　September ○　　　October ○

MY OBSERVATIONS

What I can see:

_____

_____

_____

_____

What I can smell:

_____

_____

The weather is:

_____

_____

More common St John's wort plants are similar to the flax-leaved type, but they mostly have more obvious anthers and can grow to a height of 100 cm.

SEEN IT?

MY DRAWINGS AND PHOTOS

Flax-leaved St John's wort *Hypericum linarifolium*

Flax-leaved St John's worts have golden yellow flowers.
After the flowers die down the seed capsules split,
releasing up to 250 tiny seeds that are carried by the
wind. This plant is very rare in Britain, and is only found
in parts of North Wales and on Dartmoor in Southwest
England, and a few other scattered locations.

flower is
8–12 mm across

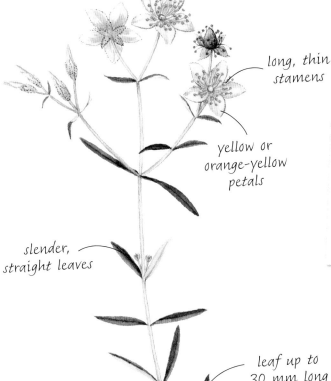

long, thin
stamens

yellow or
orange-yellow
petals

slender,
straight leaves

leaf up to
30 mm long

TYPE St John's wort family
HEIGHT Up to 30 cm
HABITAT Rocky ground
and near cliffs
FLOWERS June and July
FRUIT Brown capsule
OTHER NAMES None

RARE &
PROTECTED

July O   August O   September O   October O

83

MY OBSERVATIONS

What I can see:

_____

_____

_____

_____

What I can smell:

_____

_____

The weather is:

_____

_____

Lesser celandine is one of the first wildflowers to bloom. It provides food for insects, especially hungry bumblebees that have just come out of hibernation.

SEEN IT?

MY DRAWINGS AND PHOTOS

LOGGED IT?

Record your flower sightings at www.wildlifewatch.org.uk

I saw this flower in: March ○   April ○   May ○   June ○

Lesser celandine *Ranunculus ficaria*

Lesser celandine is a brief visitor to woodlands and other natural habitats. It grows as a patch of rosettes on the ground, topped by bright yellow flowers. However, it dies back once flowering has finished. The flowers contain between eight and 12 little petals, which only open when the sun is shining.

flower is
2–3 cm across

eight petals around
yellow stamens

heart-shaped
leaves

TYPE Buttercup family

HEIGHT 2–20 cm

HABITAT Damp woodlands and meadows, near hedgerows and by streams

FLOWERS March to May

FRUIT Rounded seed heads

OTHER NAMES Pilewort, Spring messenger

leaves are green
and glossy

BEWARE!
POISONOUS

MY OBSERVATIONS

What I can see:

_____

_____

_____

_____

_____

What I can smell:

_____

_____

The weather is:

_____

_____

MY DRAWINGS AND PHOTOS

These brightly coloured flowers were sometimes scattered over doorsteps in May. They were also used to remove warts and cure colds.

SEEN IT?

LOGGED IT?

Record your flower sightings at www.wildlifewatch.org.uk

I saw this flower in: March ○   April ○   May ○   June ○

Marsh marigold *Caltha palustris*

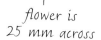

Marsh marigolds can form large clumps of deep green, shiny leaves, topped by bright golden flowers. The plants are tough and can survive in shady or sunny places, but they prefer damp soil. Marsh marigolds used to be common, but many of their marsh and bog habitats have been lost.

flower is
25 mm across

five yellow
sepals

TYPE Buttercup family

HEIGHT 20–30 cm

HABITAT Marshes, wet
meadows and damp woods

FLOWERS March to July

FRUIT Capsules

OTHER NAMES Kingcup,
Mayflower, Water-bubbles

strong,
upright
stem

kidney-shaped
leaf

BEWARE!
POISONOUS

RARE &
PROTECTED

MY OBSERVATIONS

What I can see:

_____

_____

_____

_____

What I can smell:

_____

_____

The weather is:

_____

MY DRAWINGS AND PHOTOS

The base of each Primrose petal is an orange-yellow, giving a golden centre to each flower. Many flowers grow, topping slender stalks that emerge from a central rosette of leaves.

SEEN IT?

I saw this flower in: March ○   April ○   May ○   June ○

Primrose *Primula vulgaris*

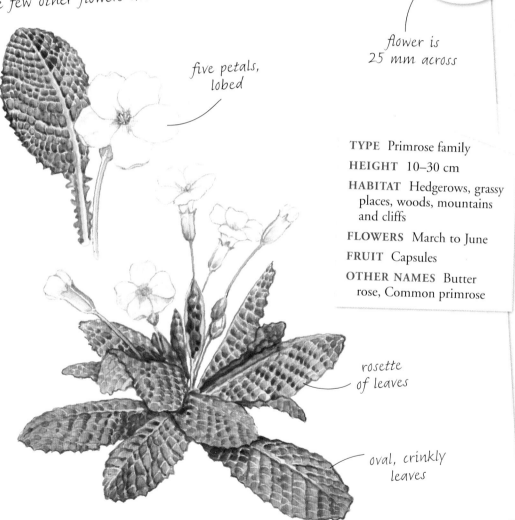

The yellow petals of the Primrose are as pale as butter, but they turn orange near their bases. Primrose's Latin name – Primula – comes from the Latin for 'first little one' and 'primrose' means 'first rose'. This is one of the early spring flowering plants that bloom when there are few other flowers around.

flower is 25 mm across

five petals, lobed

TYPE Primrose family

HEIGHT 10–30 cm

HABITAT Hedgerows, grassy places, woods, mountains and cliffs

FLOWERS March to June

FRUIT Capsules

OTHER NAMES Butter rose, Common primrose

rosette of leaves

oval, crinkly leaves

July O   August O   September O   October O   89

MY OBSERVATIONS

What I can see:

_____

_____

_____

_____

_____

What I can smell:

_____

_____

The weather is:

_____

_____

Silverweed appears in many old stories and folklore. It was regarded as a useful plant, and its leaves were even put in shoes to keep feet dry!

MY DRAWINGS AND PHOTOS

I saw this flower in: March ○   April ○   May ○   June ○

Silverweed *Potentilla anserina*

This is a creeping plant that spreads out on bare soils. The feathery leaves are divided up into many pairs of leaflets that are covered in fine, silvery hairs. Long creeping stems, called stolons, grow on the ground beneath the leaves and flowers. Silverweed has been used in herbal remedies, and its roots were used to make tea.

flower is
15 mm across

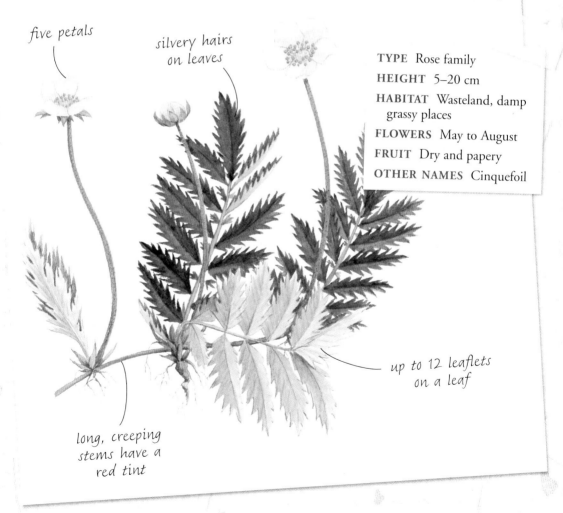

five petals

silvery hairs
on leaves

TYPE Rose family

HEIGHT 5–20 cm

HABITAT Wasteland, damp
grassy places

FLOWERS May to August

FRUIT Dry and papery

OTHER NAMES Cinquefoil

up to 12 leaflets
on a leaf

long, creeping
stems have a
red tint

July O   August O   September O   October O

MY OBSERVATIONS

What I can see:

_____

_____

_____

_____

What I can smell:

_____

The weather is:

_____

Ducks, fish and insects can hide amongst iris plants. Yellow irises remove dirt from water, and are used in sewage farms.

SEEN IT?

MY DRAWINGS AND PHOTOS

Yellow iris *Iris Pseudocorus*

Irises grow in wet places, and may even have their roots in water. They can spread by means of seeds, but also spread by rhizomes, which are swollen roots that produce buds in spring. When they spread by rhizomes, irises can quickly grow into large clumps and create a perfect habitat for pond wildlife.

flower is 9 cm across

long, slender anthers

large flowers with floppy petals

large green sepals protect flower bud

TYPE Grow from rhizomes

HEIGHT Up to 100 cm

HABITAT Wet places such as meadows, ditches, marshes and near rivers or streams

FLOWERS June to August

FRUIT Three-sided and long

OTHER NAMES Yellow flag

long, slender leaves may survive mild winters

July O   August O   September O   October O

MY OBSERVATIONS

What I can see:

_____
_____
_____
_____

What I can smell:

_____
_____

The weather is:

_____
_____

The stems of Yellow rattle have unusual black marks on them, which helps to identify this meadow wildflower. The yellow flowers are small, and protected by green bracts.

SEEN IT?

MY DRAWINGS AND PHOTOS

Record your flower sightings at www.wildlifewatch.org.uk

I saw this flower in: March ○   April ○   May ○   June ○

Yellow rattle *Rhinanthus minor*

Yellow rattle steals nutrients from its neighbouring plants. It stops grass from growing, which helps other types of wild plant to survive in meadows. At the end of the summer the seed capsules ripen and seeds inside become loose. When the capsule is shaken, the seeds rattle around, which is how the plant got its name.

flower is up to 20 mm long

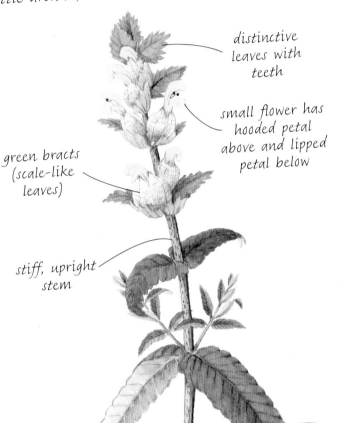

distinctive leaves with teeth

small flower has hooded petal above and lipped petal below

green bracts (scale-like leaves)

stiff, upright stem

leaves are triangular in shape, ribbed and toothed

TYPE Figwort family

HEIGHT 20–40 cm

HABITAT Open grassy places

FLOWERS June to September

FRUIT Dry capsules with seeds that rattle

OTHER NAMES Cockscomb

About Wildlife Watch

www.wildlifewatch.org.uk

If you like nature and want to find out more about the UK's wildlife then The Wildlife Trusts' new website for children and families is for you!

Log in to create a profile and start collecting nature stars for spotting real wildlife, keeping an online nature diary, or uploading your photos. The online database features more than 850 species, so you can discover loads of amazing facts about the UK's wildlife.

Make your own nature spotting sheets, play games and enjoy fun downloads. The activities database has loads of wild ideas to keep you entertained, from colouring sheets to complete, to instructions for how to make a butterfly feeder.

There's also a page for each Wildlife Trust around the UK where you can find out about nature reserves near you and discover local Wildlife Watch groups. You can also register for our monthly e-newsletter – find out Nick Baker's tips for things to do, discover our 'Beast of the month', take part in a monthly competition and much more. Just go to the website and register.

See you there!

wildlife watch · THE wildlife TRUSTS